Piano · Vocal · Guitar

EARLY JAZZ STANDARDS

781.650263
EAR

2 After You've Gone	50 My Man
6 Aunt Hagar's Blues	53 My Melancholy Baby
9 Avalon	58 Paper Doll
12 Baby, Won't You Please Come Home	61 Poor Butterfly
18 Ballin' the Jack	64 Rose Room
15 Chicago	72 Saint James Infirmary
20 A Good Man Is Hard to Find	67 St. Louis Blues
23 Hindustan	76 Somebody Stole My Gal
26 I Ain't Got Nobody	78 Sugar Blues
31 Indiana (Back Home Again in Indiana)	86 Tain't Nobody's Biz-ness If I Do
34 Limehouse Blues	90 They Didn't Believe Me
36 The Lonesome Road	81 Tiger Rag
38 Look for the Silver Lining	94 Till the Clouds Roll By
42 The Love Nest	99 Whispering
47 My Buddy	102 The World Is Waiting for the Sunrise

Cover Illustration: Ben E. Denison

ISBN 0-634-02930-4

HAL•LEONARD®
CORPORATION

7777 W. BLUEMOUND RD. P.O. BOX 13819 MILWAUKEE, WI 53213

Fremont Public Library
1170 N. Midlothian Road
Mundelein, IL 60060

For all works contained herein:
Unauthorized copying, arranging, adapting, recording or public performance is an infringement of copyright.
Infringers are liable under the law.

Visit Hal Leonard Online at
www.halleonard.com

AFTER YOU'VE GONE

from ONE MO' TIME

Words by HENRY CREAMER
Music by TURNER LAYTON

Now won't you lis-ten dear-ie while I say, __ How could you tell me that you're

goin' a - way?__ Don't say that we must part, __

Copyright © 2001 by HAL LEONARD CORPORATION
International Copyright Secured All Rights Reserved

4

5

AUNT HAGAR'S BLUES

Words by J. TIM BRYMN
Music by W.C. HANDY

Old Dea-con Spliv-in', his flock was giv-in' the way of liv-in' right.

Said he, "No wing-in' no rag-time sing-in' to - night."

Up jumped Aunt Ha-gar, and shout-ed out with all her might:

Copyright © 2001 by HAL LEONARD CORPORATION
International Copyright Secured   All Rights Reserved

AVALON

Words by AL JOLSON and B.G. DeSYLVA
Music by VINCENT ROSE

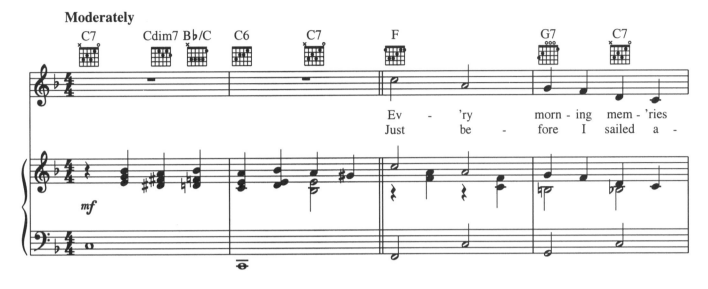

Ev - 'ry morn - ing mem - 'ries
Just be - fore I sailed a -

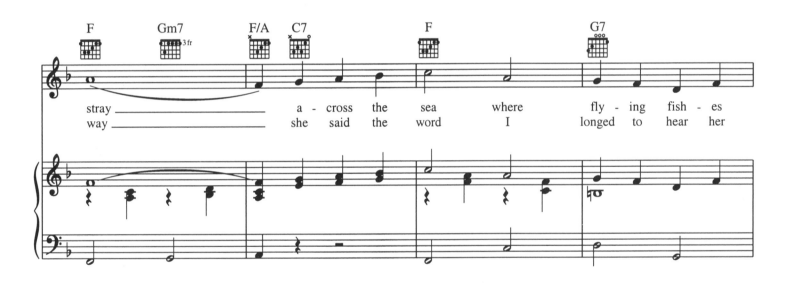

stray _____ a - cross the sea where fly - ing fish - es
way _____ she said the sea word I longed to hear her

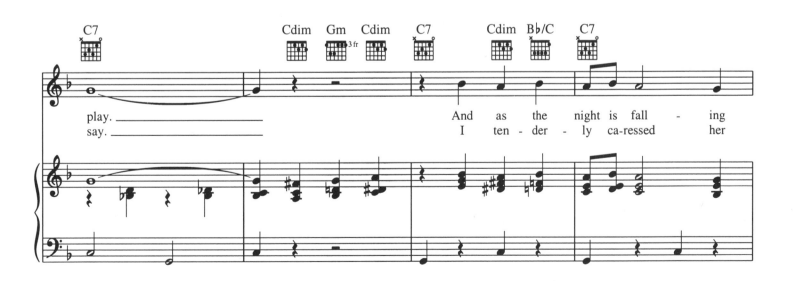

play. _____ And as the night is fall - ing
say. _____ I ten - der - ly ca - ressed her

Copyright © 2001 by HAL LEONARD CORPORATION
International Copyright Secured   All Rights Reserved

BABY, WON'T YOU PLEASE COME HOME

Words and Music by CHARLES WARFIELD
and CLARENCE WILLIAMS

Copyright © 1994 by HAL LEONARD CORPORATION
International Copyright Secured   All Rights Reserved

CHICAGO
(That Toddlin' Town)

Words and Music by
FRED FISHER

Copyright © 2001 by HAL LEONARD CORPORATION
International Copyright Secured   All Rights Reserved

BALLIN' THE JACK

Words by JIM BURRIS
Music by CHRIS SMITH

Moderately

First you put your two knees close up tight, ___ Then you sway 'em to the left, then you

sway 'em to the right, Step a-round the floor kind of nice and light, ___ Then you

Copyright © 1988 by HAL LEONARD CORPORATION
International Copyright Secured   All Rights Reserved

A GOOD MAN IS HARD TO FIND

Words and Music by
EDDIE GREEN

Copyright © 2001 by HAL LEONARD CORPORATION
International Copyright Secured   All Rights Reserved

HINDUSTAN

Words and Music by OLIVER WALLACE
and HAROLD WEEKS

Copyright © 2001 by HAL LEONARD CORPORATION
International Copyright Secured   All Rights Reserved

I AIN'T GOT NOBODY
(And Nobody Cares for Me)

Words by ROGER GRAHAM
Music by SPENCER WILLIAMS and DAVE PEYTON

Copyright © 1990 by HAL LEONARD CORPORATION
International Copyright Secured   All Rights Reserved

INDIANA
(Back Home Again in Indiana)

Words by BALLARD MacDONALD
Music by JAMES F. HANLEY

Copyright © 2001 by HAL LEONARD CORPORATION
International Copyright Secured   All Rights Reserved

LIMEHOUSE BLUES
from ZIEGFELD FOLLIES

Words by DOUGLAS FURBER
Music by PHILIP BRAHAM

Copyright © 2001 by HAL LEONARD CORPORATION
International Copyright Secured   All Rights Reserved

THE LONESOME ROAD

African-American Spiritual

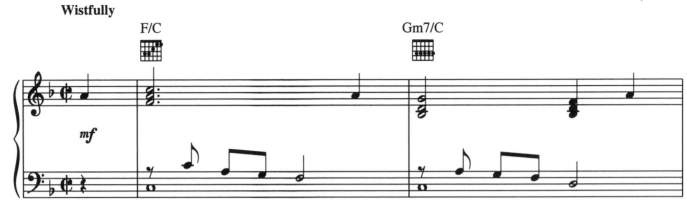

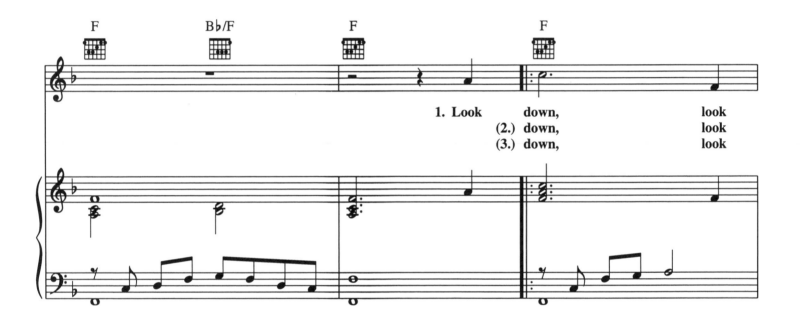

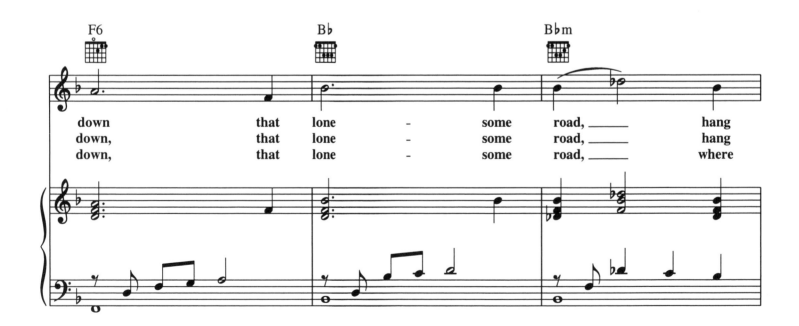

Copyright © 2001 by HAL LEONARD CORPORATION
International Copyright Secured   All Rights Reserved

LOOK FOR THE SILVER LINING

from SALLY

Words by BUDDY DeSYLVA
Music by JEROME KERN

Copyright © 2001 by HAL LEONARD CORPORATION
International Copyright Secured   All Rights Reserved

THE LOVE NEST

Words by OTTO HARBACH
Music by LOUIS A. HIRSCH

Copyright © 2001 by HAL LEONARD CORPORATION
International Copyright Secured   All Rights Reserved

43

MY BUDDY

Lyrics by GUS KAHN
Music by WALTER DONALDSON

Life is a book that we stud-y _____ some of its leaves bring a
Bud-dies thru all of the gay days _____ bud-dies when some-thing went

sigh. _____ There it was writ-ten my Bud-dy _____
wrong, _____ I wait a-lone thru the gray days _____

Copyright © 2001 by HAL LEONARD CORPORATION
International Copyright Secured   All Rights Reserved

48

49

MY MAN
(Mon Homme)
from ZIEGFELD FOLLIES

Words by ALBERT WILLEMETZ and JACQUES CHARLES
English Words by CHANNING POLLOCK
Music by MAURICE YVAIN

It's cost me a lot, but there's one thing that I've got it's my man,___
Some-times I say if I just could get a-way with my man,___
Sur cet-te terr', ma seul' joie, mon seul bon-heur C'est mon hom-me

cold and wet, tired you bet, but all that I soon for-get with my man.___
he'd go straight sure as fate, for it nev-er is too late for my man.___
J'ai don-né tout c'que j'ai, mon a-mour et tout mon cœur, A mon hom-me,

He's not much for looks, and no he-ro out of books is my man.___
I just like to dream of a cot-tage by a stream with my man,___
Et mé-me la nuit Quand je ré-ve, c'est de lui De mon hom-me.

Copyright © 2001 by HAL LEONARD CORPORATION
International Copyright Secured All Rights Reserved

MY MELANCHOLY BABY

Words by GEORGE NORTON
Music by ERNIE BURNETT

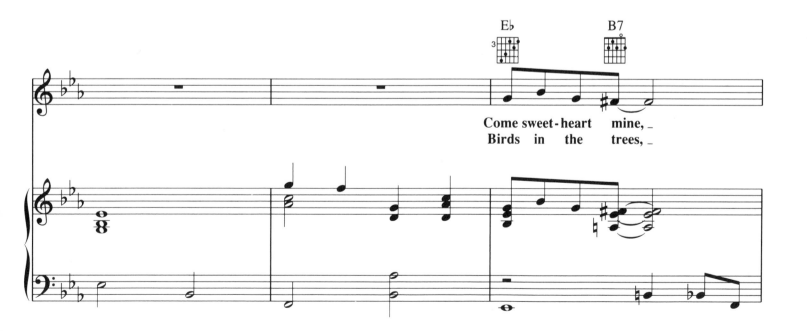

Copyright © 1990 by HAL LEONARD CORPORATION
International Copyright Secured   All Rights Reserved

or when you cry, ___ some-thing seems to grip this ver - y heart of mine.
smile thro' your tears, _ when you're sad it makes me feel the same as you.

Come to me my mel - an - chol - y ba -

by. Cud - dle up and don't be

blue. _____ All your fears are

PAPER DOLL

Words and Music by
JOHNNY S. BLACK

Copyright © 1991 by HAL LEONARD CORPORATION
International Copyright Secured   All Rights Reserved

POOR BUTTERFLY

Words by JOHN L. GOLDEN
Music by RAYMOND HUBBELL

Copyright © 1995 by HAL LEONARD CORPORATION
International Copyright Secured   All Rights Reserved

62

ROSE ROOM

Words by HARRY WILLIAMS
Music by ART HICKMAN

Copyright © 1995 by HAL LEONARD CORPORATION
International Copyright Secured   All Rights Reserved

ST. LOUIS BLUES
from BIRTH OF THE BLUES

Words and Music by
W.C. HANDY

Copyright © 2001 by HAL LEONARD CORPORATION
International Copyright Secured   All Rights Reserved

Extra Choruses (optional)

Lawd, a blonde-headed woman makes a good man leave the town,
I said a blonde-headed woman makes a good man leave the town,
But a red-head woman makes a boy slap his papa down.

O ashes to ashes and dust to dust,
I said ashes to ashes and dust to dust,
If my blues don't get you my jazzing must.

SAINT JAMES INFIRMARY

Words and Music by
JOE PRIMROSE

Copyright © 1992 by HAL LEONARD CORPORATION
International Copyright Secured   All Rights Reserved

SOMEBODY STOLE MY GAL

Words and Music by
LEO WOOD

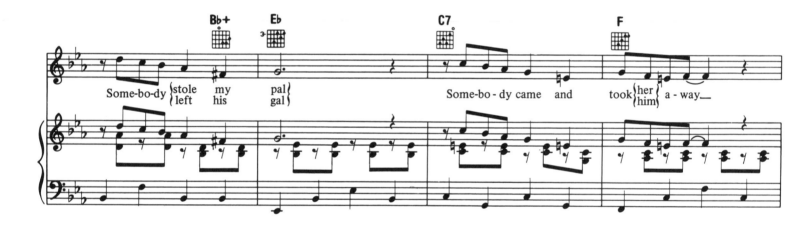

Copyright © 2001 by HAL LEONARD CORPORATION
International Copyright Secured   All Rights Reserved

SUGAR BLUES

Words by LUCY FLETCHER
Music by CLARENCE WILLIAMS

Copyright © 2001 by HAL LEONARD CORPORATION
International Copyright Secured   All Rights Reserved

TIGER RAG
(Hold That Tiger)

Words by HARRY DeCOSTA
Music by ORIGINAL DIXIELAND JAZZ BAND

Copyright © 1994 by HAL LEONARD CORPORATION
International Copyright Secured   All Rights Reserved

TAIN'T NOBODY'S BIZ-NESS IF I DO

Words and Music by PORTER GRAINGER
and EVERETT ROBBINS

Copyright © 2001 by HAL LEONARD CORPORATION
International Copyright Secured   All Rights Reserved

89

THEY DIDN'T BELIEVE ME

from THE GIRL FROM UTAH

Words by HERBERT REYNOLDS
Music by JEROME KERN

Copyright © 2001 by HAL LEONARD CORPORATION
International Copyright Secured   All Rights Reserved

TILL THE CLOUDS ROLL BY
from OH BOY!

Words by P.G. WODEHOUSE
Music by JEROME KERN

Copyright © 2001 by HAL LEONARD CORPORATION
International Copyright Secured   All Rights Reserved

WHISPERING

Words and Music by RICHARD COBURN,
JOHN SCHONBERGER and VINCENT ROSE

Copyright © 2001 by HAL LEONARD CORPORATION
International Copyright Secured   All Rights Reserved

THE WORLD IS WAITING FOR THE SUNRISE

Words by EUGENE LOCKHART
Music by ERNEST SEITZ

Copyright © 1994 by HAL LEONARD CORPORATION
International Copyright Secured   All Rights Reserved

Classic Collections Of Your Favorite Songs

arranged for piano, voice, and guitar.

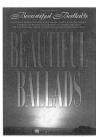

Beautiful Ballads
A massive collection of 87 songs, including: April In Paris • Autumn In New York • Call Me Irresponsible • Cry Me A River • I Wish You Love • I'll Be Seeing You • If • Imagine • Isn't It Romantic? • It's Impossible (Somos Novios) • Mona Lisa • Moon River • People • The Way We Were • A Whole New World (Aladdin's Theme) • and more.
00311679 ....$17.95

Irving Berlin Anthology
A comprehensive collection of 61 timeless songs with a bio, song background notes, and photos. Songs include: Always • Blue Skies • Cheek To Cheek • God Bless America • Marie • Puttin' On The Ritz • Steppin' Out With My Baby • There's No Business Like Show Business • White Christmas • (I Wonder Why?) You're Just In Love • and more.
00312493 ....$19.95

The Best Standards Ever Volume 1 (A-L)
72 beautiful ballads, including: All The Things You Are • Bewitched • Can't Help Lovin' Dat Man • Don't Get Around Much Anymore • Getting To Know You • God Bless' The Child • Hello, Young Lovers • I Got It Bad And That Ain't Good • It's Only A Paper Moon • I've Got You Under My Skin • The Lady Is A Tramp • Little White Lies.
00359231 ....$15.95

The Best Standards Ever Volume 2 (M-Z)
72 songs, including: Makin' Whoopee • Misty • Moonlight In Vermont • My Funny Valentine • Old Devil Moon • The Party's Over • People Will Say We're In Love • Smoke Gets In Your Eyes • Strangers In The Night • Tuxedo Junction • Yesterday.
00359232 ....$15.95

The Big Book of Standards
86 classics essential to any music library, including: April In Paris • Autumn In New York • Blue Skies • Cheek To Cheek • Heart And Soul • I Left My Heart In San Francisco • In The Mood • Isn't It Romantic? • Mona Lisa • Moon River • The Nearness Of You • Out Of Nowhere • Spanish Eyes • Star Dust • Stella By Starlight • That Old Black Magic • They Say It's Wonderful • What Now My Love • and more.
00311667 ....$19.95

Classic Jazz Standards
56 jazz essentials: All The Things You Are • Don't Get Around Much Anymore • How Deep Is the Ocean • In the Wee Small Hours of the Morning • Polka Dots and Moonbeams • Satin Doll • Skylark • Tangerine • Tenderly • What's New? • and more.
00310310 ....$16.95

I'll Be Seeing You: 50 Songs of World War II
A salute to the music and memories of WWII, including a year-by-year chronology of events on the homefront, dozens of photos, and 50 radio favorites of the GIs and their families back home, including: Boogie Woogie Bugle Boy • Don't Sit Under The Apple Tree (With Anyone Else But Me) • I Don't Want To Walk Without You • I'll Be Seeing You • Moonlight In Vermont • There's A Star-Spangled Banner Waving Somewhere • You'd Be So Nice To Come Home To • and more.
00311698 ....$19.95

Best of Cole Porter
38 of his classics, including: All Of You • Anything Goes • Be A Clown • Don't Fence Me In • I Get A Kick Out Of You • In The Still Of The Night • Let's Do It (Let's Fall In Love) • Night And Day • You Do Something To Me • and many
00311577 ....$14.95

Big Band Favorites
A great collection of 70 of the best Swing Era songs, including: East of the Sun • Honeysuckle Rose • I Can't Get Started with You • I'll Be Seeing You • In the Mood • Let's Get Away from It All • Moonglow • Moonlight in Vermont • Opus One • Stompin' at the Savoy • Tuxedo Junction • more!
00310445 ....$16.95

The Best of Rodgers & Hammerstein
A capsule of 26 classics from this legendary duo. Songs include: Climb Ev'ry Mountain • Edelweiss • Getting To Know You • I'm Gonna Wash That Man Right Outa My Hair • My Favorite Things • Oklahoma • The Surrey With The Fringe On Top • You'll Never Walk Alone • and more.
00308210 ....$14.95

The Best Songs Ever
80 must-own classics, including: All I Ask Of You • Body And Soul • Crazy • Endless Love • Fly Me To The Moon • Here's That Rainy Day • In The Mood • Love Me Tender • Memory • Moonlight In Vermont • My Funny Valentine • People • Satin Doll • Save The Best For Last • Somewhere Out There • Strangers In The Night • Tears In Heaven • A Time For Us • The Way We Were • When I Fall In Love • You Needed Me • and more.
00359224 .... $19.95

Torch Songs
Sing your heart out with this collection of 59 sultry jazz and big band melancholy masterpieces, including: Angel Eyes • Cry Me A River • I Can't Get Started • I Got It Bad And That Ain't Good • I'm Glad There Is You • Lover Man (Oh, Where Can You Be?) • Misty • My Funny Valentine • Stormy Weather • and many more! 224 pages.
00490446 ....$16.95

Prices, contents, and availability subject to change without notice.
Some products may be unavailable outside the U.S.A.

FOR MORE INFORMATION, SEE YOUR LOCAL MUSIC DEALER,
OR WRITE TO:

HAL•LEONARD™
CORPORATION
7777 W. BLUEMOUND RD. P.O. BOX 13819 MILWAUKEE, WI 53213

www.halleonard.com

0201